Big Thoughts from Little Golfers

Big Thoughts from Little Golfers

Memorable Quotes during Youth Golf Lessons

Nicole Weller
Illustrated by: Jennifer Zivoin

nicole weller

Big Thoughts from Little Golfers

Published by Gatekeeper Press
2167 Stringtown Rd, Suite 109
Columbus, OH 43123-2989
www.GatekeeperPress.com

Library of Congress Control Number: 2021932455
ISBN (paperback): 9781662909191
eISBN: 9781662909207

Dedication

To...

My husband Ty #teamweller!

My family stateside and overseas.

My mom, Rosemarie... thanks Mom!

My close friends and industry colleagues.

Pixabay Images

All parents and grandparents who will understand many of these random comments with an appreciative and knowing smile.

Schaffer Robichaux, 3D Cloud

And most importantly...

The countless excited youngsters who play golf a little or a lot:

This book is because of you and how you see life so refreshingly every day!

Foreword

I've been involved in the game of golf for all but four years of my life as a D-1 collegiate competitor, student, coach, instructor, golf craft leader, duo PGA/LPGA national award winner, maintenance crew worker, outside range and cart attendant, clubhouse kitchen cook, shop attendant, assistant professional, head teaching professional, golf bride, Girls Golf Site Director, national summit presenter and more. I wouldn't trade my experiences for anything and am so truly grateful for the travel, relationships, and adventures that have come about all through golf.

Many of my most treasured memories come from working with youngsters, from those who try golf for the first time to the ones who play competitively. What especially leaves an impression are the heartwarming, random, and refreshingly innocent truths that erupt from them at any given moment. Many followers and friends have encouraged me to write a book compiling the feel-good quotes I post on my social media – so if you are in need of a smile, I hope some of these remarks will help with that!

#socialkindness

The Book

I've combined fun and engaging tips on how parents/ grandparents/mentors can help effectively guide youngsters as they discover both new life skills and how golf fits in. With a master's degree in sport psychology/ motor skill learning, I am sharing that all ages and stages of life have their own styles and timeframes for how and what is learned.

Keep in mind the overall age of the children and their current social, emotional, physical abilities, attention-spans, thinking abilities, and their definition of 'fun' (your definition might differ). This is about their own personal experience to discover in their own way (just like you already learned your way)...your goal is to create the environment for their self-discovery.

Children learn through play, games, and activities; combine those with learning tools that suit their current learning needs, just like how kindergarten and college classrooms are set-up based on student needs at various stages of education.

Let children do their best; it doesn't have to be just 'adult right' at the moment, they have plenty of time to develop! This is about sparking a fun interest and learning about movement and coordination, not perfecting skills yet.

I hope you enjoy some of these youngsters' spot-on remarks and moments as much as I have!

"The inspiring message and quotes in Big Thoughts from Little Golfers are actually useful for all ages of golfers. Nicole helps you feel good about the game!"

Pia Nilsson / Lynn Marriott VISION54

"A perfect book to remind us about the simplicities and joys of life through the eyes of children!"

Kay Cornelius, 2012 LPGA
National Youth Golf Leader

"Big Thoughts from Little Golfers is a great read for both children and parents offering creative and easy-to-understand ideas for parents helping their children get into the game, while keeping a strong focus on fun and positivity."

Michelle Holmes, U.S. Kids
Golf Master Kids Teacher

Adventures in Full Swing

Nicole's Swing Notes for Mentors...

For two to three-year-old children, use oversized lightweight plastic kick balls, 3-inch plastic ball pit balls and foam balls and have them mimic:

- Two thumbs ('thumbies') to the grass
- Feet under each ear (feet on visual aids like footprints)
- Elephant's trunk swing motion or a 'One-Two Back and Through' motion.

For four to five-year-old children, use 3-inch plastic ball pit balls and real golf balls to demonstrate and encourage:

- Hands together as a team, thumbs down front of handle to grass
- Feet under each shoulder (on visual aids like footprints)
- Ball in middle of feet, Letter Y Arms and Club
- 'One (*backswing*), Two (*forward swing*), Show My Shoe!'

Coach, look, I just hit a ball into the air and it looks like yours but farther!!

Six-year-old boy after learning how to hit basic iron shots... **I can now do it gooder!**

When you nail a drive 100 yards off your knees with a very short student driver and the five-year-old student comments (complete with eyeroll)... **That was lame-o.**

Five-year-old sporting a wicked reverse grip that could hit it nearly 100 yards with roll... **Finally, driver time, so I can hit the smack out of it!**

A new girl golfer was making her swing and in the middle of the backswing said... **Did you know that I'm having a sleepover with my Grandma?** *Well, I didn't but I do now, thanks for sharing and oh, nice shot!*

Five-year-old about to hit drivers with some oversized light kick balls...

Me: Are you so ready?!?

Him: YES!! I could do this FOREVER!

Quote from a student as we explored The Grip...

Me: Cool, I'm good with that grip.

Student: I'm not (smiling)!

Seven-year-old boy selecting a VISION54 practice activity card about feeling the texture of the grip during the swing (and me expecting something back like 'soft' or 'rough'):

Me: Well, how did that grip texture feel during the swing?

Him: Greasy.

Older student who hit a less-than-desirable shot...

It wasn't going well, so in the middle of the swing I tried to do Emergency Procedure #47. Didn't work.

Seven-year-old boy after hitting a gorgeous wedge shot 30 yards high into the air:

Am I just the best seven year-old student you have?

Seven-year-old girl just returning to golf and practicing showing off her back shoe sole in her swing finish...

So sad the front shoe doesn't get to show off. The back shoe is The Movie Star of the whole swing.

Five-year-old student after pacing off his drive in twenty-two giant steps...

I hit my drive twenty-two minutes away!

Six-year-old girl when asked what she'd like to do in the lesson...

I think I'd like to start with putting today and then do some ironing.

Six-year-old boy:

Me: Great job with putting, let's head over to do some big hits.

Him: Oh, did you know that 'Big Hits' is my middle name?

Me: No, no I did not. How cool!

Seven-year-old at a return range lesson:

Wow, is that tree new?

Photo Location: The Landings Club Deer Creek Course,
Savannah, Georgia

Ten-year-old girl who doesn't get to play much golf...

Me: Cool shot, nice swing!

Her (as she tees up the next shot): Thanks, it's a gift.

The moment when a six-year-old student lights up like a Christmas tree when he learns he just drove the ball 83 yards, drops his club, runs to go tell his dad, trips, tumbles onto the grass and somersaults right into his run again until he reaches his dad with his animated tale.

Four-year-old during a range learning game...

Yah, I don't think this is working out too well for me.

Okay then, onto Plan B!

Nine-year-old girl shot imagination...

Me: What's your target, where is this ball headed?

Her: Down the clubhouse chimney (over 400 yards away) and into somebody's water glass, of course!

Well, of course!

Six-year-old boy speaking while hitting balls at the same time...

Yah, I usually don't listen to what coaches tell me to do. I just do it my way and it's better.

Nine-year-old student learning about golf swings and shots with Birdie Ball equipment...

This is so much fun... the day just keeps getting better and better!

When an eight-year-old student actually
lets out a **"Yippee"** DURING every shot of the
entire session.

Six-year-old student talking away while
hitting his driver and right in the middle of his
swing asks:

**Hey Coach Micole (with an M)... watch this shot
but have you thought about your plans yet
for Halloween?**

Older youngster who realized he only practices
from the best lies which didn't help him develop
his overall game, just sterile flat-lie range shots:

Hello, my name is ... and I'm a Range Fluffer.

Adventures in Putting

Nicole's Putting Notes for Mentors...

For two to three-year-old children, use fun colorful golf balls and allow for open exploration with these guidelines:

- Two thumbs ('thumbies') to the grass (split or reverse grips fine for now!)
- Feet under each ear (feet on visual aids like footprints)
- 'Tick Tock Swing the Clock' pendulum motion

For four to five-year-old children, demonstrate:

-  Two thumbs down front of handle (split or reverse grips fine for now!)
- Feet under each shoulder (on visual aids like footprints)
- Ball in the middle of feet, Letter Y with arms and club
- 'Tick Tock Swing the Clock' pendulum motion

During a girl's class when a golfer read her putt twice saying,

I know I already read the green but I wanted to make sure it didn't change in the last two minutes.

Three-year-old girl, while putting...

Her: Are we going to fly a kite today?

Me: Well, I didn't have that planned for today but it would be fun!

Eight-year-old seeing how many two-putts out of five chances she could make from ten feet away from the hole...

But what if I get a one sinker?

Six-year-old new golfer...

Me: Would you like the flagstick in or out?

Him: I'll take the flagstick out so there's more room for my golf ball!

Five-year-old observation on very large indents in the green while we were finding and fixing ball marks...

I bet a gator came up and chomped the grass!

Eight-year-old suggestion to me while putting the 'Tic Tac Toe – Three in a Row' game and my ball went past the intended middle box to the back middle one...

Him: Good try. Can I give you some feedback?

Me: Thanks, sure!

Him: You should go for the middle box, then it's free play to any other spot.

Me: Good idea, thanks!

Seven-year-old playing a game of Putting School (various advancing levels called grades)...

Wow, I'm really in second grade in regular school but here am in sixth grade now... I'm on FIRE!

While playing 'Rockets to Earth' putting game, one youngster was a bit baffled when we cleaned up and didn't realize we had cleaned up the circle (Earth) and asked...

Oh no, where is Earth?

Four-year-old student replacing a flagstick cautiously, not letting it go for what seemed like forever...

I wasn't sure if it's stable.

Seven-year-old student wisdom on letting unwanted memories go...

Me: Does it matter what the putt is for if you're giving it your best anyway?

Him: No, not really.

Me: What would you do if the memory of what it's for won't leave you alone and you don't like that?

Him: Easy, I'd just knock off the memory!

Ten-year-old new golfer...

Me: Do you like playing this Putting School game with grade levels?

Him: Oh Yes! I would pay much more to do this kind of school than my regular school.

Photo Location: The Landings Club Deer Creek Course, Savannah, Georgia

Five-year-old student while we're playing Tic Tac Putt...

I think I can putt my ball between those two and into the last box when I use my Magic Touch.

Adventures in Chipping

Nicole's Chipping Notes for Mentors...

For two to three-year-old children, use oversized plastic ball pit balls, foam balls and/or standard golf balls, allowing them to explore chipping with:

- Two thumbs ('thumbies') to the grass
- Feet under each ear (feet on visual aids like footprints)
- 'Tick Tock Brush the Grass' phrasing

For four to five-year-old children, note chipping is like putting with:

- Two thumbs down front of handle
- Feet under each shoulder (on visual aids like footprints)
- Ball in the middle of feet, Letter Y arms and club
- 'Tick Tock Brush the Grass' phrasing

Quote from a very young man who chipped it too far over the green...

Yes, that swing was big like a strong storm!

The moment when you ask a youngster if the target needs to be moved closer (thirty-five yards away) and he says yes and runs to move it closer.... by one foot, before proudly running back, beaming.

Five-year-old student...

Me: Do you think you can chip a few out of these five balls into the chipping square?

Him: Oh, I think I can manage it.

The moment when you ask a ten-year-old student if she can chip it closer to the hole than your chip and she says **"100% YES!"** *and then does.*

The moment when a seven-year-old student is checking if her chip made it inside ten feet of the hole with a tape measure and she says, **"Yes, dilly dilly!"**

Adventures in the Sand

Nicole's Sand Notes for Mentors*...

For two to three-year-old children, use oversized colorful plastic ball pit balls and/or foam balls and very basic sand concepts including:

- Two thumbs ('thumbies') to the sand
- Dig, dig, dig those feet into the sand!
- Big hit!

For four to five-year-old children, explore the following ideas:

- ⦿ Two thumbs down front of handle
- ⦿ Dig, dig, dig those feet into the sand!
- ⦿ Mighty Swing, Splash the Sand! *(Splashboard with small sand mound helpful for early success!)

The moment when a seven-year-old student throws his hat off and out of the bunker stating, **"This hat impairs my full vision"** before continuing to excavate his ball out of the sand.

Eight-year-old student:

Wow, this is a lot of good sand! as he proceeds to just pop it out effortlessly near the flagstick.

Four-year-old boy while drawing art with his finger in the sand and when asked what the swirls and twirls were to him, said...

My art teacher said this is like...art. It's a beautiful something about nothing.

Animal Adventures

Nicole's Notes for Mentors Regarding Animals in Golf...

This is a great time to discuss which animals make their homes on the course, safety around animals, and how rules might be affected by them...make it fun!

- One fun idea is to incorporate learning about animals into golf activities like dry erase or crayon drawings of a golf course with items including an animal who lives there (turtle, alligator, squirrel, bird, bug, deer, fox...).

- For warm-up, stretch imitating how animals move and sound. Some youngsters really enjoy being able to move and make the related noises they're learning about in life.

'What If' moments...

Me: If you could be any kind of animal, what would it be?

Him: Well, definitely not an ant, cuz you could get squashed.

Top three most intriguing things to a four-year-old during a golf lesson...

1. Bugs

2. Broken golf balls

3. Boo Boo's and Band Aids

Five-year-old while discussing sending the ball up in the air like a butterfly that just passed us...
I can draw good butterflies. I'm a butterfly making machine!

Five-year-old girl...

Her: You know what there are so many sand gnats around us?

Me: No, why?

Her: Cuz they're attracted to the sparkly necklace on me!

Ah ha, case solved!

Running non-stop commentary from a six-year-old boy...

Me: How was July 4th?

Student: I went swimming and there were bats trying to swoop down and scoop me up! Oh, there's a bee over there. He's saying 'Don't get close to me.'

Me: Really? How can you tell? I don't speak 'Bee.'

Him: Oh, I know Bee language a little. Did you know a dragonfly eats 50 flies a day? I learned that on Harvey TV. I love that show.

Four and five-year-old campers...

Me: So is everyone enjoying camp this week?

Boy 1: Oh yes, yes! I like it one hundred and ninety nine times!

Boy 2: Well I like it 1,000 times!

Boy 3: I like it 1,000 times plus 1,000 puppies!

Discussion about summer gnats with a six-year-old boy...

Me: Well, do you know why they're really here?

Him: No, why?

Me: Well, maybe they play Bug Golf and want to get better, just like you!

Him: Really? Their clubs must be so much smaller than their arms. Maybe they have fourteen clubs too.

As a former Wake Forest Demon Deacon student-athlete, the moment your young student announces that he has a new black and gold fish who he's named Wake (Forest).

From a five-year-old student who drew a dinosaur for me...

Me: That is such a cool dinosaur! Is it a Brontosaurus?

Him: No Coach, it's a Brachiosaurus!

Get with it Coach, it's obvious!

Five-year-old riding back to the range in the cart with me from a course adventure....

WOW! That big bird just flew right by me, I'm so glad he didn't poop on my head.

Four-year-old student...

Me: Name three animals who make their home on the golf course.

Her: A deer, a cowapiller (caterpillar) and.... a dolphin.

Boys in a six-through-nine-year-old golf class...

Me: So what does it sound like when you hit that shot just the way you like it?

Student 1: Well, it kind of sounds like hitting a cow.

Student 2: Or a cow bell.

Adventures on the Course

Nicole's Course Notes for Mentors...

Getting kids out onto the course safely early on is a vital part of showing them what our game is about: basically moving a ball towards and into a hole across a diverse landscape.

Most sports enthusiasts learn and train in the same environment in which they've played (tennis, basketball, soccer...). Golf practice and play are done in different places and I've heard several comments from youngsters who thought golf was just something that happened at the range or putting green. Kids like and need to move around; their attention spans and bodies at this age crave movement and a variety of activities as they learn about life... moving through a hole or two allow for that.

You'd beat my dad by 97 strokes because he keeps hitting trees.

From one young man to another as they inspected some flowers near the course...

You'll want to plant either 4 o'clocks or Sweet Peas, as they smell very pleasant and are annuals.

Six-year-old quote...

A long time ago when I was younger, I used to miss the ball a lot more.

When a family of four is coming up onto #9 green and the kids run off the green in the middle of playing while parents still putting to tell you that one (age four) hit a **"big hit seven iron"** *and the older brother made a* **'hole in two' on a par three.**

Random remark from a student during play, in the middle of his 'pre-shot routine,' nonetheless...

Did you know my nanny runs in marathons?

The moment you're serenaded with a holiday song by a six-year-old while driving back from the back range to the clubhouse and are about to thank him.... as he then boldly launches into verse two.

The moment when, in the middle of a half-hour session on number ten green, a five-year-old student putts and then out of nowhere drops his putter and runs up to give you a long hug saying...
I'll miss you when I leave today ☹

Six-year-old girl who really loves golf and has very developed skills for her age, meeting for first time with Dad to see if we'd like working together...

Me: What has been your proudest golf moment so far?

Her: Making eagles are my bestest thing!

Ten-year-old national competitor working with me that day on a course challenge...

Me: So we're playing a match play format today for a few holes in which we can't hit the green in regulation (three-stroke penalty for this game) but have to see where is the best 'leave place' to still make par. Other player gets to choose short game club/shot. First hole is a par four, remember we can't hit the green in two.

Him: OK, then I'll just hit it in one.

Five-year-old who just hit his first drive over a twenty-five yard creek, follows by sailing another one then nearly forty-five yards over the creek...

Me: Wow, how did you do that, that was amazing?!

Him: Well, it was such a stronger hit...

Nine-year-old golfer strategy after being asked if he was five years old, how would he get over a creek with a short driver... he took a moment, looked at it and said...

Easy, I'd just putt it across the bridge.

Four-year-old student...

Me: So what made you happiest during our golf today?

Girl: My heart!

Me: Oh nice! Why so?

Girl: Because it's my most strong power.

The moment when a new-to-golf nine-year-old wants another lesson right away, visits again the next day and then proceeds to drain a twelve-foot putt and a seventeen-foot putt during her first round of golf!

Eleven-year-old boy just finishing his first time ever on a golf course and as we're leaving a lagoon hole, he stops, turns around and runs back onto the green yelling...

Wait! I need to soak up how beautiful this all is!

Four-year-old riding by a house with a moving truck and many cars on our way back from the course to the range...

Me: Hmm, I wonder where they're moving to or from?

Student, crinkling his nose and thinking hard: Ummmm, France?

Eight-year-old girl about to hit over a little water and bunker with a six iron...

Me: So which golf ball do you want to hit for this shot, this old ball with emojis or the Titleist Pro V 1's?

Student: Not the emojis, they're too important.

Newly-coined phrase from a six-year-old who just learned how to use a range finder while on the course...

Let's keep playing, I want to do more Yardaging!

Six-year-old boy playing a (seemingly) simple Choice Game while riding back to the range from the course...

Me: Ketchup or mustard?

Him: Mustard.

Me: Successful chef or superstar NBA player?

Him: Superstar NBA player.

Him: Would you rather watch Auburn play Georgia or Falcons play Mississippi State?

Me: Ummmm...hang on, let me jump into a whole new level here!

Eleven-year-old on how his competitive play style is either total focus for the entire round or hops in and out of focus as needed...

I'm in and out but need to extend my battery life and focus more.

Adventures
with Food

Nicole's Notes for Mentors Regarding Food...

Having early discussions about healthy foods can be quite fun through golf! Here are a few fun games to play:

- **Eat the Rainbow**: Discuss foods that are the same colors as the rainbow.

- **Food Alphabet** (ages 4-5): Youngsters are just learning about letters. Name a food and discuss what letter that word ends in. Sound it out. Pick the next food that starts with that letter. This game may last a few minutes or much longer.

  Example: Egg. Grape. English muffin. Noodle.

- Get some **food flashcards** and make up a story or discuss the pictures.

- **Paper Bag Snack Pack**: What healthy foods would a child decide to put into his or her golf snack bag? Use crayons or markers to draw the front of a paper bag (can make a hand puppet out of it) with the types of foods that might go inside.

Four-year-old learning 'Did You Know' - Filling our Happy Tank (intrapersonal skill development)...

Me: So what are some things you think of to fill up that Happy Tank when needed? *(Thinking he'd say maybe a pet or family member or favorite toy...)*

Young Man: Goldfish crackers!

Quote about the 'five second rule' on dropped food....

It doesn't count for chocolate, it's timeless ☺

Six-year-old boy I noticed having something yellow stuck to his forehead as he bounded up the hill to the back range...

Me: Hi there! You seem to have something yellow stuck to your forehead... Is it part of an egg?

Him: No!

Me: Is it.... Play Doh?

Him: Nope!

Me: I give up, what is that?!?

Him: Fruity Pebble Cereal! *(Which he then locates and peels off to inspect)*

Quote from a new and exciting four-year-old student as we're getting to know each other during our introduction interview...

Him: Did you know I'm so strong because I eat my broccoli?

Me: Why no, I did not! Do you have any brothers or sisters?

Him: No, I just have Me.

Four-year-old joke...

Him: Want to hear a joke?

Me: Ok, bring it on.

Him: How does a nut sneeze?

Me: Hmm, I'm 'nut' sure. Tell me.

Him: Ca-Shew, Ca-Shew!

Four-year-old Thanksgiving camper:

Me: So what icing design would you like for me to make on your brownie? *(thinking he'd say maybe a star or swirl...)*

Him: A ninja.

Conversation with a three-year-old boy:

Me: So, how was Halloween?

Him: Gweat!

Me: What did you dress up as?

Him: Captain Hook

Me: What did you like best?

Him: My favorite part was the goldfish. I like them better than candy. And whole grain, of course.

Seven-year-old comments about protein snacks that he would eat to keep his energy up on the course...

Me: So what kinds of foods would be good energy protein to bring during your golf round?

Him: Steak!

Me: But how would you bring a steak on to the golf course?
Him: Oh, I'd just bring the leftovers.

Four-year-old joke...

Q: Why did the banana wear sunscreen?

A: Because it might peel!

In helping encourage a student to show his rear shoe during the finish pose (adult lingo translation: rotational energy transfer towards the target), I ask 'Think on these next few swings you can Stick Your Finish and Show Your Shoe?'

Well, it's hard because I do eat a lot every day as a growing boy.

Adventures in Rules, Etiquette, & Safety

Nicole's Notes for Mentors regarding Rules, Manners, and Safety...

Golf is the perfect sports in which to teach a youngster about manners, sportsmanship, playing by the rules, with most of these extending into Life lessons and safety as well. Teach these area through games you can create while at the range or on the course. Keep it light and simple, don't overwhelm with a lot of adult rules yet.... one or two items to stay attentive to throughout the visit are perfect. Don't forget talking about sunscreen and sun protection – over 80% of skin damage happens before age 18!

- Look both ways before crossing a cart path
- Shake hands if safe and when finished playing golf. What eye color does the other person have while giving a medium squeeze?
- Help with Clean Up and leave a practice area better than you found it.
- Respect others, yourself, the game, the course and your equipment. Chat about examples in each area.

A very serious discussion amongst new golfers regarding what are some ways to respect the golf course?

Student 1: No running...

Student 2: What about if there's lightening?

Student 1: What if the lightening hits the ground?

Student 2: If it hits the ground by the hole, it might make the hole bigger?

Student 3: Yay, then we could put sand in it and turn it into a bunker!

Four-year-old girl when I asked the group to loudly introduce their names, ages and something interesting about themselves...

My name is (X), I'm five and I'm healthy a lot.

Quote from a young man while going over rules...

Me: So like golf, there are other sports and even Life that have certain rules, right?

Him: Oh yes, like 'Don't walk on your neighbor's flowers'!

Quote from a young man...

Me: Thanks for helping to clean up our ball baskets and tees from the range... let's leave a place better than we found it.

Him: Oh yah, I do that in the bathroom.

Seven-year-old girl when asked, 'So what does pace of play mean?':

No Piddling.

Five-year-old boy suggestion while taking our hats off to shake hands with our Golfer Handshakes...

I like you better with your hat on. You look gooder.

Adventures with Clubs, Equipment & Attire

Nicole's Equipment Notes for Mentors...

Playing with the **proper equipment** is key to success and wanting to stay in the game. Imagine as an adult playing with clubs that are three inches too big or wearing shoes two sizes too big but for later use... it makes things very clunky! Cutting down shafts or playing clubs that are too long while waiting to growing into them isn't ideal as those options don't account for the necessary lighter weight, more flexible shafts, and smaller grips. Youngsters should be fit by height, not age.

For youngsters ages 2-3 I've used **The Littlest Golfer First Set** shorter clubs. For youngsters roughly ages 4, I highly recommend **U.S. Kids Golf** Ultralights to get started – they allow for the 2.5-3 inches of annual average growth a child experiences and are well-designed with each demographics data in mind for weight, hand size, and more. Use the Fit Stick or

growth chart to check height... kids love to check themselves at each visit to see how much they've grown!

It's also a great time to chat about what people wear in various sports.... swimming, basketball, soccer, tennis, rodeos – have fun! What do golfers tend to wear?

When a four-year-old student digging around in the range basket of balls (and without looking up), asks...

Do you have any Pro V1's in here?

Had some tears from a five-year-old when his beloved seven iron broke in half during a shot. It was his 'favorite friend' and parting words were that it that went **"high and far but not always straight."**

Five-year-old equipment fitting discussion (almost six, very important notation, I stood corrected)...

Me: I'm going to measure your height for your clubs with my U.S. Kids Golf Fit Stick.

Him: OK, I'm five.

Me: Super!

Him: And I have 1,000 pieces of fuzzy lint in my pocket.

Me: Good to know!

Five-year-old with his new clubs, hitting his first new seven iron...

Well, this one works good.

Seven-year-old student who had learned about dress code and tucking in shirts during his first golf lesson... as we drive away on his second lesson to the course and his family is waving good-bye, he suddenly turned around and yells to those staying behind **"Don't forget to tuck your shirts in!"** *to those adults who weren't tucked in.*

Twelve-year-old boy new golfer:

Me: So what are some key items in your golf bag?

Him: Ummmmm, gum! *(As he reaches into his new bag, unzips the ball pocket and the only thing in there is... a pack of gum, from which he proceeds to unwrap a new piece and pop into his mouth).*

Six-year-old girl student showing me the differences between an ordinary white tee and an orange tee...

This tee is better for slippery golf balls and this tee is better for sturdy golf balls.

Six-year-old student's thoughts on wearing street shoes for golf since he forgot his tennis shoes...

Well, I wear tennis shoes every day but NOT really every day.

OK, that clears it up!

Quote from a two-year-old boy in a lesson as he was reading (actually very well!) his golf ball and golf club with The Littlest Golfer company brand names on them:

Him: Oh, The Littlest Golfer company.

Me: Who is the Littlest Golfer here today?

Him: That ME!

Me: You're RIGHT!

Him: You're the Biggest and Oldest Golfer.

A five-year-old boy and his new clubs...

Me: What club would you like to use?

Him: Can we use the Leader (driver)?

Adventures in Job Aspirations

Nicole's Notes for Mentors regarding Career Aspirations...

What fun it is to imagine what a youngster will grow up to be one day depending on his or her personality and interests. The following quotes show us that kids apparently have some very creative ways of looking at their future career aspirations!

Question to a young group of boys in class: What do you want to be when you grow up?

Student 1: Basketball Player

Student 2: Professional Golfer

Student 3: Doctor or Bus Driver

Student 4: Magician

Five-year-old golfer aspirations...

Me: What kind of job do you think you'd like to do as an adult?

Student: A priest or a scuba diver.

Six-year-old boy...

Me: So, what are you going to be one day?

Him: A fertility doctor. He lives near us and has a really big house, boat, and nice car, and he helps people.

Four-year-old student...

And I even know what I want to do for my jobs one day. In the mornings I'll be a doctor, in the afternoons a paramedic, on the weekends all morning and all day a doggie trainer and on my holidays, a golfer.

Seven-year-old comment when asked if he had five other twins, what would he have them do at the same time besides golf?

#1 Basketball game

#2 Swimming

#3 Be the smart studier

#4 Running

#5 Play Augusta National

Off-Site Adventures

Nicole's Off-Site Notes for Mentors...

I've been extremely honored by many wonderful recognitions throughout my career by colleagues and friends in the LPGA and PGA worlds, yet some of my favorite moments of all-time are the simple but heartfelt artwork, letters, cards and crafts I receive from young students. While at The Landings Club, I had a Wall of Fame covered with artwork that spilled over to the side of my desk, I needed more room!

While as golf coaches and instructors we can teach and guide people through improving golf skills, we also share life moments with many students that spill over outside of the course. The following stories are just a few of the many examples that show how golf and life exist everywhere, not just the course!

The moment you stop at the grocery store near work before heading home and run into a seven-year-old student in her dance outfit, who proceeds to show off some twirls near check-out. Then you take five more steps before a six year-old student yells "Hi Coach" with a big smile on his face and runs over in his baseball uniform to give you a hug before running to catch up with his Dad. Great way to wrap the day!

The moment when you receive The Invite to a four-year-old's birthday party by a youngster bouncing up and down bubbling over with excitement while she's holding onto her Mom's hand.

When you receive new artwork from students that they made with love during class or at home...

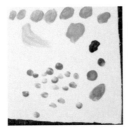

Entitled *A School of Blueberries*

An email recount from a young man's mom about where he and his 'Tee Buddy' went after visiting grandparents at the Club during his Spring break. Tee Buddies are tees with faces a youngster creates to place in ground behind their swings so their 'buddy' can keep an eye on the finish, thereby creating more goal awareness for the child.

As an aside, he has really enjoyed his golf lessons with you. At school this past week, he brought in his 'tee buddies' for show and tell and told his class all about his time with you.

An email recount from a two-year-old young man's grandmother after his first lesson in which he said no words to me during the entire half hour session but imitated all the activities. The following comments show how wonderfully fun and immersive a golf session full of putting and swinging activities can be, even for a two-year-old!

Nicole, this video was taken at dinner the day of his lesson. Though he was quiet with you, he obviously absorbed more than any of us expected☺

Here are some of his quotes, sometimes out of the blue, in the days following his lesson:

• I'm tick-tocking (with demonstration, of course!)

• Two-Hands (with 'swing' demonstrations)

• Golf Club

• Golf ball in hole

• Golf lesson with Coach Cole

For me, the icing on the cake: I read his bedtime stories on our bed the night of his lesson. When finished, he pointed to my husband's nightstand and say "Read that one!" So he and I began a new night time ritual of 'reading' and chatting about every single page of Golf Digest ☺ **Thank you from the bottom of this grandmother's heart!**

Random Adventures

Nicole's Random Notes for Mentors...

I absolutely love hearing the most heartfelt and spontaneous comments coming out of youngsters, sometimes at the most random times and even during swings! Creating an environment that allows a child to flourish safely emotionally and physically is vital to creativity and future interest in that activity.

As coaches, we always try to find ways for parents, grandparents, and mentors to better help their youngster. Wanting to help a child always comes from a good place in the heart to make things better and faster yet it unfortunately and unintentionally stifles individual growth. I encourage adults to allow a child to find his or her own way of doing something at first - to have their own personal First Experience. Creating an environment in which you can help guide them to finding their own answers is the best way; research shows that when someone is shown another's way of how to do something, the recipient doesn't learn and own it as well as when they discover the 'Ah-Ha' moment by learning it themselves. This is further supported by a T.R. Armstrong experiment in 1970 measuring how augmented (external) feedback supports performance while it is present, but can create dependency thereafter. Watching failure about to happen is hard and can pull on one's heart strings; however a person must fail and make mistakes in order to learn. Helping a child create a Mistake Ritual provides a way to acknowledge the mistake, refocus, and move on. Mistakes are good; bring them on for learning as long as the child is safe.

The Positive Coaching Alliance is a wonderful resource that we utilize to become better coaches for both youngsters and their families. We observe the following types of family coaching at times and offer ideas on how to make the family experience even better.

- Bulldozer / Lawnmower: A style in which the adult clears the path for the child so no mistakes are made or to avoid failure and all that it brings, limiting decision-making and emotional recovery skills needed to be learned by the child for sport and life.

- Joysticker: A style in which an adult moves a child or puts swing motions into 'correct positions' as deemed right by the adult instead of letting children find it themselves, making them more and more reliant/dependent on outside feedback and positioning instead of self-discovery and self-reliance.

- Helicopter: A style in which an adult constantly hovers over and near the child making comments or giving instruction during play or practice to create an 'adult-correct' result.

Anne Walker is one of the top college coaches in the country. She has guided the Stanford Cardinals to four consecutive NCAA Championships berths, and captured the first national title in program history during the 2014-15 season.

In a Positive Coaching Alliance article listed on the PCA website, Walker describes the evolution of sports parents from being Helicopter Parents (who always have a close watch over their kids), to Velcro Parents, to Bulldozer Parents. To Walker, "Bulldozer parents do all the work for their kid because they don't want them to get hurt. They push all problems out of their kid's way so their kid doesn't experience hardship. By doing this, though, kids not only avoid problems, but also miss learning crucial life lessons. As a result of Bulldozing, when faced with issues such as not making the starting lineup, kids will go to their parents rather than finding a strategy or putting forth more effort to succeed, which can be problematic. Walker brings this to the attention of all parents so that they can avoid this behavior and instead let their kids experience hardship so they can learn how to solve problems on their own."

Request from a young man...

Can you help me tie my shoe? My mom isn't that good.

When a five-year-old looks up at you quizzically asking what the crowd of people and cameras are doing there and you answer "**Filming.**" *Then you catch the look and say* "**Video'ing.**"
Much better.

Commentary from some younger brothers from the same family with same parents...

Brother #1: Coach, did you go to Wake Forest University?

Me: I sure did...

Brother #1: Well, my Mom went to Wake Forest.

Younger Brother #2: Well MY Mom went there too!

Five-year-old student...

Him: Do you know why I just beat you in a blinking contest?

Me (eyes watering): **No, why?**

Him: I can not blink the whole day long, even forever.

In an effort to learn where visiting students are from, I asked, 'So, where does everyone live?'

Well, we live in a hotel.

A speech by one clever young lady after earning her recognition:

I'd like to thank my legs for supporting me, my arms for being at my side and my fingers that I can always count on!

Nine-year-old boy...

Coach Nicole, I'm so glad you moved to NC so we could meet!

Brief speech from a camper...

I'd like to thank my Dad, my coaches, the chef and myself.

Quote after a lesson with a seven-year-old visitor on vacation with her family for the first time in Pinehurst...

I want to move here now because that's where my new golf coach is!

Observed a major discussion during camp regarding Santa and The List...

Girl: Well, I have a lot of things on my list.

Boy: Oh, you can only have three wishes.

Quote from a wonderful six-year-old going to a birthday party after our lesson...

Me: Let's head over to the putting green, we're having a golf party over there.

Him: Oh wow, now I'm going to TWO parties today... a golf party AND a birthday party. This is the best day of my life!

Six-year-old young man while practicing some golf...

My girlfriend is a little shy, she's younger than me.

Very serious quote from a camper during his acceptance speech...

I'd like to thank my mind, my club, my parents, and my coaches.

Six-year-old boy on his long life story...

When I was in Mommy's tummy I lived in (names state), **then I was born in** (names another state**) and then we moved here. Day, day, day, day, day, day, day...... and now here we are. That's my whole life, I think.**

Five-year-old boy discussing colors...

Me: I like dark blue, not quite like my pants today, these are a little lighter.

Him: But in the dark they'd be dark blue.

Seven-year-old student arriving for his morning lesson...

I was sleepy in the car over here this morning but was so excited when I got here that I woke right up and couldn't wait!

Nine-year-old student...

I'm going to be the big 1-0 this year!

Four-year-old boy...

Me: What's your favorite color?

Him: Green!!

Him again: But I also like yellow second.

Him again (but coming up very close to whisper in my ear): **And I have to whisper to you that I also really like red too!**

Six-year-old girl helping as a regional conference demo student for coach participants...

Dad: Thanks for helping today. I think Coach Nicole really appreciated it!

Girl: Do you think it was the time of her life?

The moment when a five-year-old runs back from his car during pick-up to bring you a flower.

Six-year-old boy commenting on my art golf club I had just crafted out of Bristle Blocks...

Hmm, you could use some work on that.

Four-year-old comment as we were counting team scores up in response to what was ten plus eleven is and he has apparently only learned to ten, so far:

Well, there are only ten (numbers), so that's it.

Two four-year-old twin boys:

Me: What's your favorite number?

Twin 1: Eleven. It's more than 4, which is how old I am.

Me: And how was your run down and up that big hill?

Twin 2: Super, it was a very long trip though.

Eight-year-old boy...

Him: Just had my birthday. Turned eight!

Me: Happy Birthday!! Do you feel any different all of the sudden at age eight?

Him: Yes, I feel a little taller today.

*The moment when a four-year-old boy leaves golf class at the end of the day, runs back for a hug and then while pulling away in the golf cart with Dad, waves and yells **"I Love You!"***

The moment when a ten-year-old guest visiting her grandmother does three deep yoga breathes during warm-up while you each share one thing you appreciate at that moment and she says...

Being able to visit with you three days during my trip instead of just two.

Returning six-year old annual student...

I remembered golf because I have a great 'rememory'!

The moment when a twelve-year-old climbs out of the car, waves while getting his clubs out of the trunk and runs up to the tee, smiling, saying...

I was so happy when my Mom picked me up from school and said I had lesson with you today. What club do we start with?

Five-year-old student from Youth Holiday Camp...

It's the best thing in the world!

The moment when a five-year-old from the morning class returns to the Club for dinner, sees you and runs past your high five hand to go straight in for a hug.

Quote during camp...

Camper: Coach Jim, why are you on THAT other team?

Coach Jim: It evens out the teams or it wouldn't be fair.

Camper: Well, but Coach Jim, you're worth like 10 people, so THAT'S still not fair.

Four-year-old...

Me: What are you thankful for over the Thanksgiving holiday?

Him: The earth. You want to know why?

Me: Sure!

Him: Because if we didn't have an earth, we'd be floating around everywhere in space.

Me: Good point!

When a six-year-old walks right up to you before class and says,

Did I tell you that I actually have two loose teeth?

In Closing...

Thank you to all parents, grandparents and adult mentors who give of themselves to make the life of a child better... the memories will last their entire lives and much of it because of you!

I hope you enjoy the positive interactions and comments that come out of mentoring and encouraging a person who is just beginning to see the world and all that it has to offer. Seeing things in life for the first time through a child's fresh experience is truly remarkable and refreshing.

Surveys and research show that FUN is the #1 reason a youngster participates in an activity... enjoy your time together and I hope you receive some of the most endearing and heartfelt comments and quotes as I have ☺

Happy Golfing!

#socialkindness

About the Author...

Introduced to the game of golf at age four by her Swiss father Max, Nicole played in numerous national youth and amateur events before playing D1 golf at Wake Forest University and graduating with a Bachelor's Degree in psychology. Following a Master's Degree in sport psychology/ motor skill performance from the University of Tennessee and presenting at conferences such as the World Scientific Congress of Golf at The University of St. Andrews, Nicole has served students in many wonderful locations including Cherokee C.C. and Fairways & Greens Golf Center in Knoxville, Tennessee, The Landings Club on Skidaway Island in Savannah, Georgia, U.S. Kids Golf Academy at Longleaf Golf & Family Club and the Pinehurst Golf Academy at Pinehurst Resort. Nicole and her PGA husband Ty currently reside in Pinehurst with their cat, Jada.